LC 10/2017

The Christmas Story

From the King James Bible

According to the Gospels of Matthew and Luke

Paintings by Gennady Spirin

HENRY HOLT AND COMPANY

NEW YORK

The Gospels are four books that tell the life of Christ and his teachings. They are found in the New Testament of the Bible.

The Gospel of Saint Matthew comes first, followed by the Gospels of Saints Mark, Luke, and John.

Saint Luke tells the story of the angel Gabriel's visit to Mary with the news that she would give birth to Jesus. Luke also tells about the journey to Bethlehem, the birth of Jesus in a stable, and the visit by the shepherds.

Most scholars believe that Luke was a physician. Some say he was also a painter. He traveled around the ancient world with Saint Paul, spreading the teachings of Christ. Many think Luke wrote his Gospel while living in Greece or Asia Minor seventy to eighty years after Christ's death and resurrection. He is considered to be the author of another book in the New Testament, the Acts of the Apostles. Of the four Gospel writers, he provides the most complete account of the circumstances of Christ's birth.

Matthew was one of Jesus' disciples. It is likely he wrote his Gospel fifty to seventy-five years after Christ's death and resurrection. Matthew believed the birth of Jesus fulfilled a prophecy in the Old Testament: "Behold, a virgin shall be with child, and shall bring forth a son, and they shall call his name Emmanuel, which being interpreted is, God with us" (Matthew 1:23). Matthew's Gospel provides the story of the three wise men. Like Luke, Matthew traveled to many places in the ancient world and preached about Jesus.

AND IN THE SIXTH month the angel Gabriel was sent from God unto a city of Galilee, named Nazareth,

To a virgin espoused to a man whose name was Joseph, of the house of David; and the virgin's name was Mary.

And the angel came in unto her, and said, Hail, thou that art highly favored, the Lord is with thee: blessed art thou among women.

And when she saw him, she was troubled at his saying, and cast in her mind what manner of salutation this should be.

And the angel said unto her, Fear not, Mary: for thou hast found favor with God.

And, behold, thou shalt conceive in thy womb, and bring forth a son, and shalt call his name Jesus.

He shall be great, and shall be called the Son of the Highest: and the Lord God shall give unto him the throne of his father David:

And he shall reign over the house of Jacob for ever; and of his kingdom there shall be no end.

7

Then said Mary unto the angel, How shall this be, seeing I know not a man?

And the angel answered and said unto her, The Holy Ghost shall come upon thee, and the power of the Highest shall overshadow thee: therefore also that holy thing which shall be born of thee shall be called the Son of God.

And Mary said, Behold the handmaid of the Lord; be it unto me according to thy word. And the angel departed from her.

II

Then Joseph her husband, being a just man,
and not willing to make her a public example, was
minded to put her away privily.

But while he thought on these things, behold, the
angel of the Lord appeared unto him in a dream,
saying, Joseph, thou son of David, fear not to take
unto thee Mary thy wife: for that which is conceived
in her is of the Holy Ghost.

And she shall bring forth a son, and thou shalt
call his name Jesus: for he shall save his people from
their sins.

Then Joseph being raised from sleep did as the
angel of the Lord had bidden him, and took unto
him his wife.

13

14

And it came to pass in those days, that there went out a decree from Caesar Augustus, that all the world should be taxed.

And all went to be taxed, every one into his own city.

And Joseph also went up from Galilee, out of the city of Nazareth, into Judaea, unto the city of David, which is called Bethlehem (because he was of the house and lineage of David),

To be taxed with Mary his espoused wife, being great with child.

16

And so it was, that, while they were there, the days were accomplished that she should be delivered.

And she brought forth her firstborn son, and wrapped him in swaddling clothes, and laid him in a manger; because there was no room for them in the inn.

20

And there were in the same country shepherds abiding in the field, keeping watch over their flock by night.

And, lo, the angel of the Lord came upon them, and the glory of the Lord shone round about them: and they were sore afraid.

And the angel said unto them, Fear not: for, behold, I bring you good tidings of great joy, which shall be to all people.

For unto you is born this day in the city of David a Saviour, which is Christ the Lord.

And this shall be a sign unto you; Ye shall find the babe wrapped in swaddling clothes, lying in a manger.

And suddenly there was with the angel a multitude of the heavenly host praising God, and saying,

Glory to God in the highest, and on earth peace, good will toward men.

22

And it came to pass, as the angels were gone away from them into heaven, the shepherds said one to another, Let us now go even unto Bethlehem, and see this thing which is come to pass, which the Lord hath made known unto us.

And they came with haste, and found Mary, and Joseph, and the babe lying in a manger.

And when they had seen it, they made known abroad the saying which was told them concerning this child.

And all they that heard it wondered at those things which were told them by the shepherds.

But Mary kept all these things, and pondered them in her heart.

And the shepherds returned, glorifying and praising God for all the things that they had heard and seen, as it was told unto them.

24

Now when Jesus was born in Bethlehem of Judaea in the days of Herod the king, behold, there came wise men from the east to Jerusalem,

Saying, Where is he that is born King of the Jews? For we have seen his star in the east, and are come to worship him.

When Herod the king had heard these things, he was troubled, and all Jerusalem with him.

◦

And when he had gathered all the chief priests and scribes of the people together, he demanded of them where Christ should be born.

And they said unto him, In Bethlehem of Judaea: for thus it is written by the prophet,

And thou Bethlehem, in the land of Juda, art not the least among the princes of Juda: for out of thee shall come a Governor, that shall rule my people Israel.

Then Herod, when he had privily called the wise men, enquired of them diligently what time the star appeared.

And he sent them to Bethlehem, and said, Go and search diligently for the young child; and when ye have found him, bring me word again, that I may come and worship him also.

When they had heard the king, they departed; and, lo, the star, which they saw in the east, went before them, till it came and stood over where the young child was.

When they saw the star, they rejoiced with exceeding great joy.

And when they were come into the house, they saw the young child with Mary his mother, and fell down, and worshiped him: and when they had opened their treasures, they presented unto him gifts; gold, and frankincense, and myrrh.

The *wise men* and the shepherds spread the good news of Christ's birth, and today, on December 25, we celebrate that important occasion. But December 25 is not the actual anniversary of Christ's birthday. No one knows the exact date of his birth. Many scholars believe that before the fourth century, his birthday was honored on January 6 and called the Nativity. Also on that date, a festival, Epiphany, celebrated Christ's baptism and the wise men's visit to the stable in Bethlehem. It was not until A.D. 353 that Pope Liberius in Rome declared December 25 a Christian holiday to mark the birth of Christ.

At Christmas, we light candles to rejoice in the light that Christ brought into the world.